*AZU's Dreams of Vietnam
Hanoi*

Published in 2007 by
AZU Editions (Thailand) Ltd.
111 SKV Building, 8/Fl
Soi Sansabai, Sukhumvit Soi 36
Klongton, Klongtoey
Bangkok 10110
Thailand

Tel: 66 (0)2 712-4016
Fax: 66 (0)2 661-2894
office@azueditions.com
www.azueditions.com

ISBN 978-974-8136-54-7

Printed in Malaysia

Copyright 2007
AZU Editions (Thailand) Ltd.

All rights reserved. No part of this publication may be reproduced, stored in a retrieval system or transmitted in any form by any means, electronic, mechanical, photocopying, recording or otherwise, without the prior written permission of AZU Editions (Thailand) Ltd. All content, text, illustrations, and photographs in this publication are protected by national and international trademark and copyright laws. Any infringement of the rights of AZU Editions (Thailand) Ltd. may lead to prosecution without warning.

For information about reproduction rights to the photographs in this book, contact AZU Editions (Thailand) Ltd.

Cover: The One Pillar Pagoda is one of Hanoi's favourites.

AZU'S
DREAMS OF VIETNAM™

Hanoi

Photographs by Martin Reeves
Text by John Hoskin

AZU

Previous spread: A bird's-eye view of the city, with West Lake in the foreground.

Left: Chinese temples, traditional Vietnamese hats, and bicycles remain defining images.

Like a spider
at the centre of its web,

Hanoi dominates the Red River Delta, from where it has long served as Vietnam's focal point. Not always the country's capital, it is nonetheless the nation's historical and cultural heart.

In 1010 AD, Prince Ly Thai Tho sought to establish the capital of a new dynasty and affirm Vietnam's independence from China. While travelling along the Red River, so legend has it, he saw a dragon preparing to take wing. This he took as an auspicious sign and decided he could find no better location for his city.

So was born Thang Long, 'Soaring Dragon,' Southeast Asia's oldest surviving capital. Over the centuries the name changed, to Dong Kinh, from which the Europeans derived their name for northern Vietnam, Tonkin, and finally, in 1831, to Ha Noi, 'City Within the River.'

Attractively characterized by lakes, parks, and trees, Hanoi is primarily distinguished as a historic city. In recent years, new and refurbished hotels and restaurants, and arts and craft shops have added a modern appeal, but it is the legacy of the past that captivates. If no dragons are now likely to appear, still the legendary and the mythical define the main sights.

Indeed, legend lies at the very heart of one of Hanoi's most popular areas, Ho Hoan Kiem,

Above left: The dragon, depicted at Ngoc Son Temple, is associated with the legendary founding of Hanoi.

Right: Hoan Kiem Lake is at the heart of Hanoi both spiritually and physically.

'Lake of the Restored Sword.' Here, in the fifteenth century, it is said that a magical sword fortuitously appeared and was used to vanquish Chinese invaders. Afterwards, a tortoise rose from the lake, snatched back the sword, and returned it to the watery depths.

And so the people credited the spirit of the lake with their victory, and in its celebration they erected the three-storey Tortoise Pagoda on a tiny island in the middle of the water. Today, Ho Hoan Kiem is an oasis amid the bustle of the city, and on its banks old folk perform tai chi exercises in the early morning.

In a similar vein, the ornate Quan Thanh Pagoda was built in honour of Tran Vu, guardian spirit of the north, who defeated an evil serpent,

Above left: Giant tortoises are recurring motifs at the Temple of Literature, one of the city's most important ancient sites.

Right: A huge drum in the grounds of the Temple of Literature, which is dedicated to Confucius.

a tortoise, and a nine-tailed fox that had been terrorizing the area.

Mythical creatures exist not only in legends, but also become manifest in the decorative details of several pagodas. The tortoise motif, for example, is encountered at what is perhaps Hanoi's single most fascinating shrine, the Temple of Literature. Founded in 1070, the walled and multi-courtyard temple is notable equally for its architecture and for its original function as Vietnam's first university. Precious amongst the temple's artifacts are 82 engraved stelae resting on the backs of stone tortoises.

Goddesses, too, played a part in Hanoi's history, and the beautiful little One Pillar Pagoda was constructed by Emperor Ly Thai Thong after Quan

An, Goddess of Mercy, had appeared to him in a dream and prophesied the birth of a long-desired male heir.

Myths and ancient history add colour and curiosity to Hanoi's individual sights, but it is recorded history that accounts for the face of the city, lined and wrinkled in part, but full of character and ever-changing expressions. Thus, exploring the streets is to be constantly surprised by districts as diverse as the former French Quarter with its colonial villas and leafy boulevards, and the Old Quarter comprised of a maze of narrow streets that once formed the city's commercial hub.

Wonders also extend beyond Hanoi to Halong Bay, famous for its 3,000-odd rock outcrops that rise dramatically from the sea to create a scene as

Above left: Shouldering their wares, street vendors are typical figures in the urban landscape.

Right: Hanoi today is a city of eclectic architectural styles.

Left: Beyond Hanoi, island-studded Halong Bay offers its own wonders.

Following spread: More and more cars and motorcycles crowd the city streets as prosperity increases.

haunting and as lovely as a Chinese brush painting.

Of course, here, too, there was a dragon. Halong Bay translates as 'Descending Dragon' and the story is that a dragon's footsteps dug deep valleys in the earth as the creature was returning from the mountains to the sea. When it finally plunged into the water, the sea rose, filling the valleys and turning the mountaintops into islands.

Fanciful it is, but totally enchanting.

Previous pages:
*Architectural sights range from the classical (**left**) to the simply curious (**right**).*

Above and right:
Built in 1911 and modelled after the Paris Opera, the neo-classical Opera House was a glittering focus of social life in the French colonial era.

Previous spread:
The Presidential Palace, once the residence of the French governor-general of Indochina, is now used for official functions.

Left: *Designs for modern city traffic.*

Above: *More traditional traffic.*

Left: *Venerable colonial villas can still be seen in Hanoi.*

Above: *Cyclo drivers ride past the beautifully restored Metropole Hotel.*

Previous pages: *Bicycles and mopeds (**left**) are the transport of choice, while cyclos (**right**) are the traditional taxis.*

Left: *Ho Chi Minh's Mausoleum, in the square where the revolutionary hero declared independence in 1945.*
Above: *Heroic statuary in the Soviet Realist style.*

Left: *The ornate entrance to Quan Thanh Temple, dedicated to Taoist religious belief.*

Above: *Colourful and fanciful decorative detail adds to the exoticism of Hanoi's venerable temples.*

Following pages: *Lake views, with both ancient and modern sights, are characteristic of central Hanoi.*

Left: *Quiet moments in the lush park surrounding Hoan Kiem Lake.*

Above: *Lakeside parks are favourite spots for tai chi exercises in the early morning.*

Left: *The two-tiered entrance archway to the venerable Temple of Literature.*

Above: *Crusty tiled roofs and curling eaves once defined the city skyline.*

Above: *Buddha images are enshrined in niches decorating the tower of Tran Quoc Pagoda.*

Right: *With its origins dating back to the sixth century, Tran Quoc Pagoda stands on a tiny peninsula of Hanoi's West Lake.*

Following spread: *The city panorama with the Red River in the distance, seen from the Sofitel Plaza Hotel.*

Left and above: *Flowers sold on the streets add a splash of colour to the urban landscape.*

Following pages: *There is a brisk trade in fresh produce such as sugar cane (**left**) and limes and chillies (**right**), sold at street stalls and open markets.*

Left: *An engraver of wooden stamps works from his street-front shop.*

Above: *Smiling faces on masks sold during the Tet celebration, the traditional Vietnamese New Year.*

Left: An orchestra of traditional musical instruments accompanies water puppet performances.

Above: Water puppetry is a unique theatrical art that traces its folk origins back to the twelfth century.

Left: *Halong Bay is a veritable wonderland of some 3,000 islets dotted over an area of 1,500 square kilometres.*

Above: *The prow of a boat carved in the form of a dragon adds to the mythical aura of Halong Bay.*

Following spread: *The serene beauty of Halong Bay at sunrise.*

Hanoi

Travel Facts

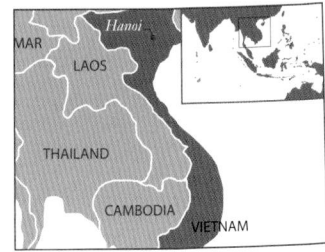

Where It Is

Hanoi is in the north of Vietnam, about 100 kilometres from the Gulf of Tonkin, and about 200 kilometres south of the Chinese border. The city is located on the right bank of the Red River. It is 1,760 kilometres north of Ho Chi Minh City. Its geographical coordinates are 21 degrees North, 105 degrees East.

How To Get There

By Air
Most visitors to Hanoi arrive at Noi Bai International Airport, which is 35 kilometres north of the city. Regional and international destinations include Bangkok in Thailand, Kuala Lumpur in Malaysia, Luang Prabang in Laos, Hong Kong, and Singapore.

By Train
There are daily train services between Hanoi's main station and cities to the south including Hue and Nha Trang. The coastal rail route goes all the way to Ho Chi Minh City in the south. There are also train services to Lao Cai in the northwest, from where it is possible to travel on to China.

By Road
Bus services connect Hanoi with regional towns and cities in the north, as well as coastal destinations to the south such as Hue, Danang, Hoi An, Nha Trang, Dalat, and Ho Chi Minh City. There are also bus services to Vientiane, Luang Prabang, and Savannakhet in Laos.

When To Go

Hanoi's weather is usually agreeable all-year round, with no particularly bad months to avoid. The humid, tropical climate is characterized by monsoons, as is the case in most of northern Vietnam. Generally there are two main seasons: the hot, rainy season and the cool season, which also sees some rain.

The hot, rainy season, which is usually considered as summer, runs from May to October/November. There is plenty of rain during these months, with an average temperature of ninety degrees Celsius. The most sweltering month of the year is June.

The 'winter' season from November to March/May is cool, with an average temperature of seventy degrees Celsius. These months are mostly dry, but some rain can be expected. January is the coolest month. The transition months of April and October are noted for variable weather conditions.

The tourist season runs from June to August and from October to Tet, the New Year festival in January or February when transport and accommodation is difficult to book. The best time to visit is from February to April and from September to November. The official high season is from September to April.

Find Out More

Comprehensive information can be found at the Vietnam National Administration of Tourism's excellent website **www.vietnamtourism.gov.vn**. For more general information go to **www.vietnamtourism-info.com/english**, **www.hanoi.gov.vn/eng** or **www.guidevietnam.com**.

Above: The cubist design of Ho Chi Minh's Mausoleum was envisaged as a symbol of eternity.

Acknowledgements

The publisher would like to thank the following, whose assistance has made this book possible:

Ramita Saisuwan and Eric DiAdamo.

Authors

Martin Reeves *is a British photographer who has been based in Southeast Asia since 1990. He has travelled extensively throughout the region documenting culture, travel, and lifestyle. His work has been frequently exhibited both locally and internationally.*

John Hoskin *is an award-winning freelance travel writer who has been based in Thailand since 1979. He is the author of many highly acclaimed books on travel, art, and culture in Southeast Asia, and has had over 1,000 magazine articles published.*